River of
Awe

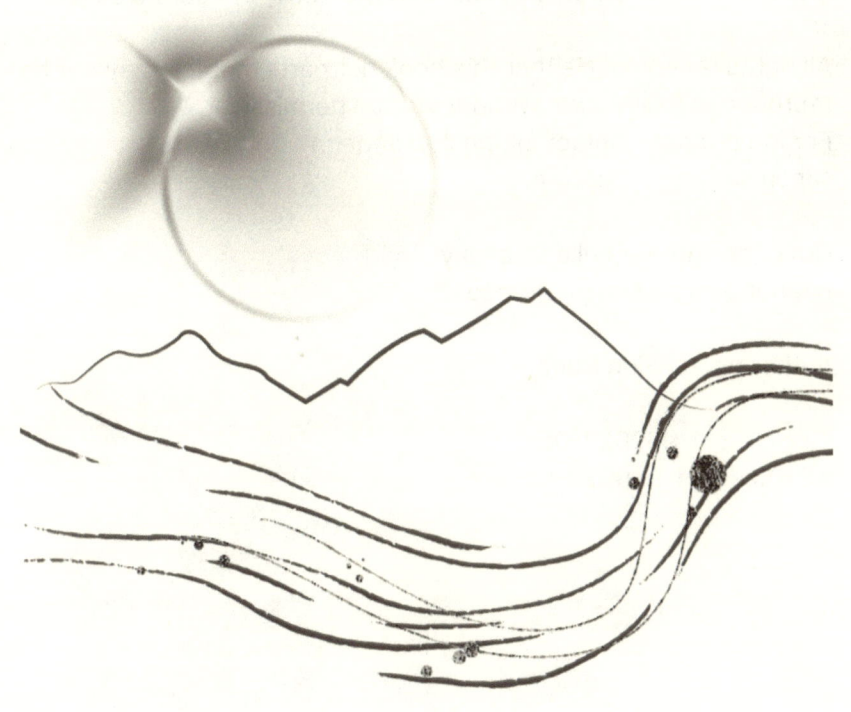

POEMS & INQUIRY FOR THE HEART'S PATH

LAURA WEAVER

River of Awe
First Published in 2025
Copyright 2025 © Pamela Hale, and the family of Laura Weaver.

Cover design: Michelle Stransky
Interior design: Marcia Breece

Author photo: Finn Dugan

ISBN: 978-1-969023-05-7
eISBN: 978-1-969023-06-4

CONTENTS

THREE:
on the riverbank

FOUR:
surrendering
to the flow

FOREWORD

BY PAMELA HALE, LAURA'S MOTHER

This book is a collection of poems written by Laura Weaver, many of them in the last year of her life. We, her beloved family, have put the collection together to fulfill one of her deepest wishes.

The poems are untouched. With the family's help, I have written reflection questions as we believe Laura would have done and arranged the poems in sections to mirror the architecture of her first book of poems, *Luminous*. We've included some poems she considered unfinished that we could not leave out and also included a list of poems she wanted to write and include. And, as a prelude to her poetry, we've included an essay Laura intended to be the first post in a blog she had planned to begin. It is a powerful statement about our need for the Divine Feminine in today's culture. Restoring a balance between feminine and masculine energies would be good medicine for the dis-ease running through our culture. Laura saw her cancer as both personal and a metaphor for the suffering in the collective.

We miss Laura greatly, every day. And yet, as the journey with grief progresses, deep sadness and pain begin to transform into gratitude for all she represented and all she taught us. In fifty-five years, Laura led a big life and touched a huge circle of people. Her professional bio is impressive. First a creative writing teacher at University of Colorado, she moved on to work with Passageworks, co-authoring the book *The Five Dimensions of Engaged Teaching*, which has been used in countless international teacher trainings-leaving a legacy to those advancing social and emotional learning in schools. In her work with the American Leadership Forum, Laura took strong stands for racial equality, led wilderness trips, and facilitated retreats with a sophisticated and skilled group of leaders.

On a personal level, the Laura we knew loved to dance and sing, sit in council, have her head rubbed, walk the land, sweat in powerful lodges, walk the coastline, cuddle with friends, hike the mountains, play with her adult children, take selfies in nature, walk again, drink good tequila, have deep conversation, draw oracle cards, lie on the earth, drink red wine, travel to sacred places, ask how your heart is, study with spiritual teachers, walk the land again, drink tea, tell her truth, swim with whales and dolphins, watch for hawks, light candles, sit in the sun, circle with women, talk to the ocean, trek to her most sacred Blue Lake, consult the ancestors and unseen beings, read great thinkers, and write, write, write.

She adored her children. Simon Alexander and Mariah Alexander, who are the two out of three biggest reasons it was so hard for her to leave the earth plane. Meeting her granddaughter, Sofia Lily Alexander, was the fulfillment of her fondest wish. Not being able to be physically present as a long-term grandmother gave her the most grief.

We hope this collection of Laura's poems speaks deeply to you, and that Laura's love of life serves as inspiration for your own journey of the heart. May the river of awe flow through your life, bringing love, harmony and beauty.

Laura's family 2025

PRELUDE

SPEAKING FROM THE MYSTERY: 2018

We are a world of experts, with so many online platforms and seven-step plans. This kind of "authority" speaks from the known, from the place of having arrived somewhere.

And yet there is another voice to claim—from within us. It is a wild, untamed voice, and it streams directly from the mystery. From that part of us that is vast and deep and unknowable. From the voice within that our rational minds do not understand. This voice does not speak from a place of arrival, but from a place of Presence in the Now. And it is a voice that lives in each of us, with its own unique flavor and cadence.

It is from here that I share one strand of the cosmic story. For yes, I am a woman with an intensely personal story to offer into the cauldron of our collective memories/herstories.

And I am also a woman whose story speaks to a shadow truth that is everywhere around and within us.

All around me, I hear people speak of a particular tension they carry—on the one hand it feels as if we may be on the edge or in the midst of global climate changes we may not survive. We are in a radical apocalypse, which comes from the word "to reveal or unveil," and what has been under the surface is now being revealed.

On the other hand, we are still living amongst the skyscrapers and tenuous systems of an increasingly toxic and mechanized world. We still have to get the kids to school. And somehow there is still food on store shelves, even though the west is burning. And so, we learn to go on.

In April, I was diagnosed with metastatic breast cancer. Yes, I am well aware that this is a phrase that strikes terror in all of us. Two years before this diagnosis, I had an initial diagnosis of stage two breast cancer. I went through the impossible decision to have a double mastectomy and reconstruction. My outcomes were so positive (clear margins, no lymph involvement, and low-grade of aggression) that I was not even considered a candidate for chemotherapy or radiation. And so, on I went with my life, integrating the lessons that had come through this process.

But my life had been turned upside down, and I was still

wedded to some belief that I could get out of the upside-down world and come right side up. And though I knew there was no place to "go back to"—that I and my body and my life were forever changed—I was fully convinced that I was through this cancer journey and on to the big work of my life. The work within and without.

Through the first journey with cancer, I had engaged intensely with the stories of my female lineage—for the pattern of cancer goes back at least four generations. And if cancer is a reflection of deep old pain or dis-ease, there were many stories from that line that wanted to be heard. In particular was the story of the suppression of all that is considered feminine or female—in our personal identities, our culture, and in the world. This is not to be conflated with the body of woman—for centuries, people of all genders have been persecuted for ways they have lived with the earth, worshipped and prayed. We have all been taught to excise the "feminine"—which is generally seen as untrustworthy.

As Alberto Villoldo says—

When the first chakra is disconnected from the feminine Earth, we can feel orphaned and motherless. The masculine principle predominates, and we look for security from material things. Individuality prevails over relationship, and selfish drives triumph over family, social and global responsibility. The more separated we become from the Earth, the more hostile we become to the feminine.

We disown our passion, our creativity, and our sexuality. Eventually the Earth itself becomes a baneful place. I remember being told by a medicine woman in the Amazon, "Do you know why they are really cutting down the rain forest? Because it is wet and dark and tangled and feminine."

Though I was always fiery and rebellious, in a way I learned to construct my identity around a patriarchal ideal of success. I excelled in school and was intensely intellectual. Then, at some point in my senior year of the Bush/Reagan era—I gave all that up.

My mom tells me the story of my younger one crying out "It's not fair!" This was a kind of rallying cry my whole life—and by fair, I meant whole, life-nourishing, kind.

I had developed my own inner masculine voice, but it was a judging, critical, and vigilant voice—developed, of course, to protect the most delicate and tender parts of my being. But this kind of protection has its price.

During that first round of cancer, many things simply fell apart in my life. In a shocking upheaval a week after my second surgery, I lost a primary love relationship and my shelter—all in one full sweep. I felt intensely vulnerable, and with nowhere to live in the fierce heart of winter, I felt the call to take action and reconstruct a life of beauty. Out of this journey was a reacquainting myself, on a deeper level, with my erotic intelligence. As this awoke in me, many miracles happened in my life. Dreams I'd had for years manifested, new connections unfolded with ease, aspects of my work blossomed, and I felt I was lifting off and taking flight with new wings.

I didn't see cancer coming.

In January I began to feel some pain in my ribs—but I chalked it up to musculoskeletal issues. Then came some mild exhaustion. I got my thyroid checked out, but all seemed okay. I was working closely with my functional medicine doctor and acupuncturist, and all was well. I was feeling radiant, preparing to get my breast tattoos and celebrate the closure of that chapter of life. I had just sent my book of poems to my designer and was preparing to lead a group of beautiful souls to the Ecuadorian rainforest to connect deeply with the spirit of the forest. I was in my dharma. After fifteen years of working at a wonderful educational non-profit, new avenues were opening, and my emerging work in equity was igniting my soul.

In the rainforest, I didn't feel entirely strong. I remember feeling a little off balance and a bit tired. But the energy of the forest filled and fueled me. I was trekking through the deep mud, sitting with the kapok trees, and feeling exquisitely blessed for the opportunity to share time with two indigenous communities who had never severed their connection with the land. This remembrance of our primary connection to earth—to the wild, to the intelligence of the plant worlds—was transformative, potent, joyous. In my dreams, in our ceremonies and in my own meditations, all felt so deeply well.

I returned with some strange symptoms and went to the doctor as immediately as I could. I had pulled a hip muscle in the forest, and it didn't seem to be healing. My energy was still low. I wondered if I had a virus.

X-rays showed metastasis in my bone. And blood work showed calcium counts so high that nurses insisted I get to the hospital within the hour. From the experience of expansion—of being through the passage—I was suddenly and fiercely down a rabbit hole I had not foreseen.

I have come, through life, to call these moments sacred shatterings. Something holy, something whole, is shattered so that a new kind of wholeness can be discovered. And yet, there is no turning from the experience of the shattering. I was hospitalized for three days and three nights over a full moon Easter weekend. A map, perhaps, for this path of dying to the old and being reborn anew.

But what is the point where we could say, we've been born anew?

I have spent the last two decades steeped in rites of passage and ceremonial work of all kinds. I have found, loved, discovered, created many maps for these threshold journeys. But in a way, nothing prepared me for this encounter with Mystery, with the Unknown.

We never know. We never know how long our life will be, when our time here in this body, on this plane, will be complete. And yet, perhaps those of us who are standing in a very immediate threshold place can offer something, a voice from the wilderness. Not as an expert, but as a woman devoted to her Life, and to Life—whatever that means.

The medical world says there is no "cure" for stage four breast cancer. I know differently for I have met and spoken with dozens of people who have made this journey and are still here. My journey has been one of surrender and clear intention around my life force, this body, and this life. I have grandchildren to tend and raise, lavender to plant and harvest, wrinkles to grow and deepen, and love to give and receive.

And so, I am on a journey of healing from cancer, from a dis-ease in my cells. What I know about this is that my cells are connected to your cells. And our cells are part of the earth's body. And we are poisoning and disrespecting our earth—to such a degree that we, and the many species we live with, may not survive this era. Talk about a reckoning.

Still, I feel in my bones, yes, in my bones—that we will find a way. Because we are, in fact, remembering. And our lives depend on it—as do the lives of species who are intricately linked to the decisions we make. Terry Tempest Williams talks about the experience of witnessing the British Petroleum fires, when the ocean was quite literally aflame. At the edge of the wall of smoke and blaze, she witnessed a pod of dolphins looking at it all. Somehow, this is more heartbreaking than I know how to speak.

And the samsāric circus has gotten ever more wild, with Kardashian dramas and Greenland melting on the same scroll of headlines. What are we to pay attention to? To being anywhere but here, it seems. Because here and now means, at times, pain and discomfort. And when we slow down, when we put the phone down and the screen away, there is a void, an emptiness that we don't know how to meet.

Goddess knows we are doing our best to wake ourselves up—but why is it so easy to go back to sleep—to sip on the opiates of reality shows and materialism and vanity? Why have we chosen instead to hollow ourselves out? To numb? To look away?

I want to speak to what Terry Tempest Williams calls "Sacred Rage." It is the kind of rage that is spiritual in nature, because it stands for the sacred in all beings and all things. It is the mother protecting her child, the grandmother who is protecting the seven generations. It is we, as citizens of this planet, taking our power back from the places where we have given it away to some other agenda. No more.

I have never seen the journey with cancer as a battle or a fight. I have focused more on living at a level of balance, alignment and harmony that does not allow for cancer to exist. This, to me, is our call on the planet right now. And sometimes this means disruption.

In my journey, cancer has been a fierce disrupter of plans and patterns and habits. And I have been called to disrupt and rewire the deepest and most subtle stories operating in my very cells.

As a girl, highly attuned to the suffering of the world, I lived always with a kind of disappointment in God and life—and a vigilance around living in an unsafe world. There were intensely personal stories that contributed to setting these templates. And there were ways that I learned as a young one to override inner wisdom and to adapt. We have all been conditioned to adapt to a way of being that is profoundly unsustainable and out of balance.

The natural and innate impulse to nourish, contribute, collaborate, cooperate, cocreate—that lives in all of us—has been discredited, subverted and relegated to the trash heaps of a world that runs on the empirical and on the gross arrogance of consumerism. Eternal growth is unsustainable. And what does growth unchecked mimic? Cancer.

And so there is this profound and beautiful opportunity to remember who we are. To bring ourselves back to the circle of life, where all have a place. To restore our bodies and our earth to balance. For, lest we forget, our bodies are the earth. We not only belong to the earth, but it is our flesh and blood; it is what we are made of.

In the last decade I have sat with four close women friends who all died from cancer. Since then, I have known at least another dozen who have been diagnosed. It is an epidemic. It is a call from the feminine body—from the breasts of women. From the wombs of women. And the call says, you cannot bypass me.

In my own body, I am learning to listen ever more deeply to the wisdom here, to both what has been recorded and also what is known. There is profound intelligence, and there have been grave misunderstandings. The same kind of misunderstandings that live within us also drive the suffering in the world. Our cells carry the records not only of our current life, but of our lineage and our ancestors. This does not make us "victims" to our genetics—but it does make us libraries for books we may not even know have been written.

So many women are going through the crucible of the body, as if to remind us that mater matters. Mater/mother/existence/creation. This life is not simply about transcendence and bypassing this very physical experience. The She within all—wants to experience everything.

We have created eons of skygods. We have become Icarus flying too high toward the sun. We have forgotten the deliciousness of roots. In the rainforest, the kapok trees spread their canopies and create a micro-climate for dozens of species.

Eden has always been here for us to recognize. Our belonging is here as much as it is everywhere. Yes, we are spirits having a human experience, and this fusion of flesh and spirit is beautiful and terrible and impossible and exquisite. We are tempted to be "light chasers" who run from the dark. But there is nowhere to run to. And the darkness and the light are two sides of the face of the Divine.

Our wholeness comes from this recognition of our own nature. We can see the dark not as evil or malevolent, but rich and fertile and vibrant.

Beauty and Suffering.

ONE: **headwaters**

Zero Point

The door of the moon swings open
to the zero point
where everything is pure potential.

This, the holy moment where
your sweet "I" goes flying in the wind
like ancient prayer flags releasing
all the prayers they've held in the bones.

Here where the way of Nothing
And the way of Everything
meet in a fertile crossroads.
Here where the way of Fullness
and the way of Emptiness
are two streams from the same headwaters.

Here, where all the lineages
we have been—every role and face we've worn—
every mother-father-child-thief-zealot-saint
we've ever been is metabolized
in the ravaging light.

So that all of our struggling and grappling
and shapeshifting and yearning
and burning and turning
and seasoning and surrendering
turns back into the prima materia—
the great Stillpoint.

So that our undoing
our unbecoming
our brilliant nakedness
is our arrival point,
our new beginning—
the liberation after all
of the efforting to become.

And the I knows itself simply
as this eternal moment emerging
now as a field of sunflowers
now as a ritual of seasons rising and falling—
now as this Universe of Eyes
that is forever Seeing and being Seen.

reflection questions:
   1. How might this poem be the ultimate surrender to the Divine Mystery?
   2. What are your questions about the idea of the "zero point?"
   3. How does the poem point to the continuation of life after death?

Clearing Out the Roots

Sometimes the signs and symbols are so loud
you can't ignore them any more—
the scurrying that's been in the background
of your mind becomes a roar.
The ocean that's been dreaming you
sends visions of bigger and bigger surf.

Yes, you see that the boat of your old life
has been taking on water bit by bit—
and you finally wake up to see
the old patches aren't holding,
the boat is going to capsize, and it's time
to head to shore and build a new boat.

You've proclaimed you want a new life—
that you are the new blueprint
beyond your lineage and conditioning—
and yet the one of you who longs
for the comfort of the familiar is reluctant
to move out of the old eddy.

We are stubborn creatures, clinging
to the familiar reference points
that assure us we are the selves
we think we are. But we are also the faces
we don't recognize. There are our future selves
standing in the hallway beckoning to us—
through the labyrinths of time.

And so in comes the demolition team
to clear out the roots. At first
we are like the mule pulling against the rope—
we don't want to be dragged!
We cry out—why are you doing this to me!
God laughs—and holds up the sacred record
of our prayers—and it's in our own handwriting.

When you find the keys to your old house
no longer open your front door—
it's the good news coming for you!
For yes, there is the moment
when you stand bewildered out in the cold,
the snow falling around you,
but it is then we shapeshift from mule
to windhorse, running with the full eros
of our own awakening.

And we see what we have been resisting
is the very doorway to the evolution
we have been calling—the very invitation
we have been looking for. And here it is—
everywhere around us. Like a song
that begins quietly and then swells
and fills all of our senses

in that crystalline light of winter
you remember your own deepest prayer—
how you realigned every cell of your body
with a new song and then expected
it all to change without having to leave
anything behind. Some part of you hoped
you could keep all of your old routines.
It's so natural—to want everything that way.

But there is your future self in the doorway
saying, this old architecture is crumbling
from within you. You are growing
a new tree of life—and it requires
a different kind of nourishment.

This is not the move of the Endless Seeker
always hunting the next horizon.
Not of the unfulfilled or unsatisfied one
looking for the next intoxicating experience.
This is the one who knows the way
to build a new home inside,
on a wholly other foundation
from the one you inherited from lineage.
For this is the home you are creating
from your own Quintessence.

This is not a shelter. Nor even a place
to lay your head. You are no longer looking for that.
For you know now there is no refuge
in the way you were hoping for.
This is simply a field of grace arriving—
so you can walk out of the old house,
clear the roots, release the old vows.
So you can pour another cup of tea
and watch the sun in your own soul rise.
So, you can gather your body of light.
Dream yourself wilder and wilder
until you know the face
of the world as your own.

reflection questions:
1. What do you think is meant by "The ocean that's been dreaming you sends visions of
   bigger and bigger surf?"
2. How might your future self be beckoning you?
3. How do you see the difficulty of letting go also becoming a great gift?

WINDHORSE

This morning a windhorse came to my door—
whinnied in the deep November snow—
mane shining in the crystal light.
For just this last summer I kissed death
for the third time and returned.

And after that, a great clearing occurred—
a fierce and generous unburdening
of old attachments, cords released—
new windows in my body revealed.

The windhorse came to me to speak
to me about the emptiness of being—
not the emptiness of cold void,
but a kind of ecstatic transparency.
And together we rode out through
that deep powder, snow flying
in rainbow arcs.

There was no constriction—
no pulling away from the pain.
Nor was there hope or fear.
Just the gallop of the spirit untethered
through time, beyond time.
Just the naked openness of being
when we resist nothing—everything
awake, everything quivering with love.

reflection questions:
1. What do you imagine the windhorse represents?
2. How does "the emptiness of being" indicate a spiritual healing?
3. Can you imagine being completely open, unconstricted and alive?

THE SHAPE OF US

What shapes us has come with teeth and claws.
With nectar and the sea's own pearls.
It has come from storms and tectonic
plate shifts. From the burying of the old heart
and bearing of the new one. From the tearing
in the belly from where we were born.
From the moments when death brushes
its wing against our cheek—and then comes birdsong.

And you, western wind, you have shaped me.
When you blew me out to sea, so far I couldn't
orient anymore by shoreline. Yes, you who insisted
on many nights of solitary songs under piercing constellations,
those doorways to other ways of knowing.
You who blew in lust and power
and the passing through of many lovers.
You who dismantled me bone by bone.

And you eastern wind, who has brought sunrises
that would woo me into living again after another burn.
You would show me the faces of my elder, beckoning
to me down a path in the evening, fireflies flashing.
You who taught me about the Fool who would lead
me back to the spring where the young girl of me drinks.

And you southern wind who taught me how
to find my heart when the lightning came strong
in the night. How to go to the water and lay my body down.
How to rest in to the field of love—however
it constellates. And so here, I sleep in the aspen grove
where the deer curl in to long grass.

And north wind, riding in on the silver horse,
a crescent moon, a long shadow on the crystalline snow.
I have come to stillness with you—for you took me
to the center of the center. To that place where
there is only breath. And the song of the otherworld
like a stream flowing just along the waters of this world.
This quintessence that comes when we surrender
what we think is most essential.

This shape of us—emerging from the path itself.
To honor even the places we will never understand.
To bless that curve and edge, that wrinkle and scar,
that holy laugh that explodes out of the cracks
when the last skin is offered up.

For we are homo luminous—mud and starlight.
We do not need to run from our own humanness—
or try to scrub off its scent. It is fertile here, in the crossroads
of the infinite and mortal—it is the beautiful
crucible you came to know. Not to solve or fix,
but to listen to intimately—here in the heart
of the universe, where everything is broken and whole.

reflection questions:
1. What has shaped you on your life's path?
2. How has the shape of you "emerged from the path itself?"
3. In what ways do you see humans as "mud and starlight?" And how is this a crucible?

HUNGRY GHOSTS

It is the myth of scarcity
that is at the center of our separation disease.
And yet we are born into original generosity.
Generosity, because creation has given us
the instructions, the maps, the guidance we need.

But parts of us have forgotten,
have caused havoc with our hunger
for all that we consume but cannot taste.
For all we demand, but cannot receive.
This is why learning to receive is so essential.
It is not simply a selfish act.

To truly receive with gratitude
is to complete the cycle of endless hungers—
to know satiation, fulfillment, enoughness
so as not to blunder and ravage in desperation.

This is why stopping, simply stopping
and returning to the simple nourishment
of wind and birdsong will heal us.
This is why gratitude returns us
to knowing we are a wellspring
connected to the Wellspring
at the Center of Creation.

It is where we put our attention.
And how we face the hunger in our selves.
How we meet the ghosts in the night.
How we let the skins of illusion fly off
in the night wind. How we dive
into the eyes of the Beloved
and remember we were born
into Original Sufficiency.

reflection questions:
1. Where do you see "our separation disease" infecting us?
2. How does creation give us the guidance we need?
3. How can gratitude keep us from being "hungry ghosts?"

ORIGINAL ANCESTOR

So many ancestral lines lead
here to our becoming.
Silk roads and migrations across
the Bering Strait. Ice ages and great floods.
Starfields and the explosion of islands
in endless seas. The many singing peoples,
the many dancing peoples.
These lines of beings pouring out
from the center of the earth
from the heartbeat of stars.
Following songlines.
Forgetting and remembering.
Becoming clan and tribe.
Waving flags. Marching in wars.
Creating. Destroying.
All of this in us—in our cells
that are more space than matter
our bodies that are water
and space and starfire.

We wonder how
we have found ourselves
on a spinning planet hurling
through space—in a spinning
universe amongst universes.
The vast spaces between galaxies
mirroring the vast spaces between
the electron and the nucleus.
And through all of it—we ask
where do we come from—
who is our first mother,
our first father—who is the One
who has become the many?
This we sing from the mountaintops
and into the deep seas.
We join our song with the whalesong
that has been here for fifty million years.

What are we and how did we come
to walk here in these bodies
thinking we are the pinnacle of creation?
We so majestic and so tiny in our seeing.
So tragic in our need to devour.
And yet, when we trace all those lines back,
all of those song lines and ancestral lines
all those migration patterns and heartbeats
we find ourselves here, in the field of grace
in the heart of a mystery that is us
recognizing our own face as the face of Grace.
For grace is the original ancestor,
the one who spun us from the loom
from out of the belly of the fertile dark.
Grace is our original ancestor—
the one who sparks the fires
along the edges of the sea
and says come, gather here,
it is time you remember where you come from.

reflection questions:
1. Where do you think you came from?
2. Who were your ancestors, and who were their ancestors?
3. When you think of this cosmic remembrance, how does your heart respond?

SOMETHING IS DREAMING YOU

Down in the well,
where the holy waters sing—
something is dreaming you.

Here, where the rivers
under the rivers rise up
to meet your deepest longing.

Give up your fetish for the light
and let the fertile darkness kiss you!

Then, watch as the stars bloom
inside your every cell.

reflection questions:
1. What could be dreaming you?
2. What could be the place where "the rivers under the rivers rise up?"
3. What would it mean to "give up your fetish for the light?"

BODY OF LOVE

What if we grew bodies of love,
rather than bodies of pain?

What if these sacred vessels
were not a record of heartbreak
but the expression of our original blessing?

Not the crossroads of all the wounds and wars
but a garden seeded with the knowing of enoughness,
of true nourishment, of the honey of kindness.

What if our bodies were seeded like the acorns
of the live oaks—and if these spiral codes
opened up in us like a shower of dawn light
showing our cells the way to breathe
with the stars and drink the light of the central sun.

And what if we followed that song—
right from the beginning, that song that moves
from acorn to sapling to giant oak—
the breadth of our reach becoming
a sanctuary for the ones who come after us.

Yes what would it be to grow a body
of love from a field of belonging?
For we have carried our bodies of pain
long enough, honored them well—
given thanks to the angels of challenge
who come to soften our hard edges—
especially the ones we do not even know we have.

What does the body of pain have to say to the body of love?
What does the body of love have to say to the body of pain?

reflection questions:
1. What does your body of pain have to say to the body of love?
2. What does the body of love have to say to the body of pain?
3. What are the "angels of challenge" who have come to soften hard edges in you?

MEETING EROS

Because after the snow and the rain—
the redwing blackbirds trill in the cattails
and the song of the inner life
is born into the world again.

We emerge, like bears bounding out
of the mountain, bewildered—
blinking in the bright new light,
ravenous for the feasts of spring.

Then the seduction begins—
apple blossoms raining on wet earth,
hummingbirds unzipping cerulean sky,
the glint of streamflow and bare skin.

How the full moon pours Maylight
upon our upturned faces—
and currents flow sweet
with the spice of all that is greening.

We have died and been reborn
a thousand times for this—
to be courted by you who tears apart
the old husks and stirs the inner waters.

Yes, you, Eros—who makes us want
to eat fire and lay down in every meadow.
We have been waiting for your arrival
and now you are here—no longer

a Stranger but a Storm. You, who strikes
the bell of awakening, so the whole body
rings out. You, who pierces every part
of us with wild, delicious ache.

reflection questions:
1. How do you define Eros, and how is it defined here?
2. How might Eros court us?
3. In what moments have you felt a "wild, delicious ache?"

DREAM TEMPLE

Come to the dream temples
where the gods of healing live—
where the streams of our primal knowing
flow up from the core of the earth—
where we curl like fawns into sleep,
traveling on ships through the long night.

Become the vessel for the Great Dreamer
who casts a net into the stars to catch
the one golden fish that will speak
the language of your own particular myth,
that will teach you how to know thyself,
heal thyself, see beyond thyself.

For though in these times
so much seems impossible—
the reach of the Dreamer is infinite.
And as day dreams weave with night dreams—
we see that all that is falling away,
all that is breaking down at the end of empire
is becoming the fertile soil of the next garden.

What is awakening is some deeper medicine—
the way you can feel a river of fire
running under the cities. The way within
the steel structures of modernity
you can hear the web of roots speaking.

Come to the Dream Temples—
where we dream beyond our own small stories
for the great waves of descendants to come.
Where we join our center to the navel
of the world. And upon waking, see—
it is the future that has been dreaming us all along.

reflection questions:
1. Who is the part of you that can dream beyond appearances?
2. What greater medicine might be awakening for you now?
3. How could the future be dreaming us?

EYE OF THE WHALE

We paddle out through coral shoals—
looking for breach, for spray, for footprints
of tails on water—the sight of glistening fin.
Something has called me to this bay
for months now, across thousands of miles,
some longing for communion, for perspective.

And today I am quaking with an old fear
inside me—about my own fate,
about the fate of the earth,
about the fate of love. And I have come
to witness thousands of pounds of stardust
breaking surface, to spin in sunlight
and disappear again into the depths.

I have come to hear the stories that live
in these whale bones—pouring through
phonic lips in clicks and whistles,
in lyric melodies of primal seas and deep space.
Eons pass, civilizations rise and fall—
and still this humpback song goes on.

We see them just ahead of us now—
a mother and her calf. We come close,
but not too close—and when it is time,
slip into the sea, naked beside them—
so that suddenly the shining eye of the calf
looks into me. And for as long as I can,

I hold my breath and stay in the oracle
of this gaze that dissolves all fear.
Back in the kayak—I cannot speak.
This is what wanted to be remembered in me.
Species come and go, continents crumble,
human life like the flicker of a butterfly wing.

And yet there is this eye of awareness
looking out from the center of the milky way,
this eye of the whale imprinted
in the heart of my heart,
where stories fall away—
where even now a great silence,
that is a holy presence—
is being born.

reflection questions:
   1. If you have gone whale watching or swimming with whales, what was your experience?
   2. How does the whale represent ancient stories?
   3. How do you respond to the "eye of awareness" in this poem?

TWO: **r a p i d s**

BROKEN OPEN

Some days we fall to our knees
and pray for a new heart
that is free from the scars of this life.

For this ancient heart of ours
has been dragged around the wheel of time
behind the horse cart of suffering
for a few miles—or perhaps thousands!

There is our childhood of course—
this perfect wounding
that is passed between generations—
the pain we thought we should take on—
this pain that is not even ours.

Maybe there is even an existential
exhaustion we only notice
in the moments between sleep and waking—
an obsession with hand wringing
we can't seem to turn away from.
It all seems so personal!

Just remember—We were warned!
Our hearts were made to break open—
It was in the contract we signed just before
we tumbled down the spirit ladder.
It was in the fine print we don't ever read.

It said:
You will encounter the tumultuous winds
of your unfathomable fears
and the blooming
of your own exquisite light.

You will feel abandoned, disappointed, betrayed.
You will be asked to forgive everything—
and most of all—your own luminous self.

Your heart will break open—
and spill its mysterious treasures—
This is good news!
Don't try to stop it!

You may feel like you are on fire
with all that is awakening.
You may feel you won't make it
to the other side.

But this is your heart—
and your heart was made
to break open.

And as you pray at this altar
of your broken open heart—
you will find the handwritten note
you left yourself on the mirror
of eternity so long ago.

Note to Self:
You will have the chance
to be healed by Love.
Take it!

reflection questions:
1. Have you wished or prayed for a heart free of life's wounds?
2. Do you believe you agreed before birth to feel both tumult and ecstasy?
3 How can you take the poet's advice to be healed by Love?

SECOND ARROW

There is the first arrow—flung from the bow of life—
the pain clean and clear to the bone.
And then there is the second arrow—
the arrow we create when we cling
to our own pain, to the stories
we weave around the pain.
For we all have a crying child inside us.

There is no dodging the first arrow—
but it is the second arrow we unleash
on our own hearts—the suffering over our suffering.
This arrow we somehow want to hold onto—
to clench and hold and cradle—because it is familiar—
to play the memory over and over
like a skipped record or a ghost pain
we keep returning to.

But it is a fierce blessing to release the old ghosts
rattling around the eaves of us!
To open up the attics and basements
and let the howling One work it all out
under the moon—and then give the arrow
back to the Divine Archer!

The bitter drink of resentment dries up
the spirit and turns it to dust.
And, the blackberries are too sweet for that—
and you have plans to make a harvest wine!

Let go of that second arrow—
and all that has been waking you in the night
will settle—the pain-echoes will turn
into fireflies illuminating the sky
and you will meet the world again
with fresh eyes, with open hands.

reflection questions:
1. When have you launched that second arrow of suffering over suffering?
2. What makes you want to hang on to those second arrows?
3. Can you give the second arrow back to "the Divine Archer?"

GENEROSITY

Sometimes we need a hand up—
when we have fallen from the wagon,
face first in the mud—when we are down
deep in the belly of despair. When the dark
night of the soul has its grip—and we cannot see
our way through the endless fog.

Sometimes we need a hand up
when we are quaking in the corner
of our worst fears realized, when loss
and abandonment sit at our table,
when we are in the hold of an ache
that seems to have no end.

Sometimes we need a hand up
when the unmet children in us
are crying in the corner, running ransack
through the cupboards looking
for something to eat. Or when the adolescent
ones take the car and nearly drive
off the edge of a cliff. Or when the older
ones of us stand aloof in judgment,
behind the stacks of stories
we have collected around us.

Sometimes we need a hand up
when we have convinced ourselves
that we don't need each other—
when the Ace of Blame
and the Queen of Righteousness
are passed around the circle.
When we cannot stop and see
we are each at the table
with our own set of cards.

In heaven, which is here, which is now—
we feed and clothe one other.
We see this muddy, tear-stained One
in front of us as a version of ourselves
on another day. We each carry
and are carried for a time.
We cast no stones, no shame.
We come close enough to whisper—
I am with you.

And it is then that the god of generosity
looks out from our human eyes and
recognizes itself.

It is then we know that heaven
is not a place—but this gesture,
this open palm.

reflection questions:
    1. When have you needed a hand up?
    2. Have you ever played the Ace of Blame or the Queen of Righteousness?
    3. How might heaven be here, in the open palm?

TASTE OF WAR

She tells me how her father foraged for mushrooms
in the Black Forest—Nazis stalking him as he fled.
How after the war ended, he could never eat mushrooms again.

How primal the scent of gunpowder and hunger—
the pheromones of fear, the fierceness of love making
when we know all could be lost. And in our current moment

of the Great Story, desperate men raise flags
hoping to fill the ache with feasts of power.
But they are not sated—not with the burning

of the Amazon, or with militias that steal people
away in the night. Not with women on their arms
who have gone vacant and forgotten the curve of the moon.

Not with stealing piles of gold and wheat
and rounding up starving children
on the borders. This is a hunger that wants war.

Perhaps these men never tasted the sweetness
of the earth's milk. Perhaps beauty never cracked
the heart and tears never cleared the debris in the soul.

Instead, the charge, the threats, the posturing that rips
countries apart and builds walls against our own nightmares.
Instead, this hall of mirrors where there is only one face reflected—

for all of the others have dropped their guns and run home
to their lovers to grow gardens and bake bread.
Yes, the others have grown tired and thin

with the taste of war on the lips—a bitterness no sweet
cannot dissolve. What is it that will finally return
the war-hungry ones in all of us to the awe

of northern lights—the beacon of the pole star,
to sun on bare skin, to a moment when we knew we belonged
to something beyond the too-steady beat of machines?

For all of us remember, somewhere within,
the prayer we were born with. To be free
from the ash on the hands, to break this spell—
to run back to the forest of our own hearts, foraging
for what has been lost. So that in time,

even the most lost part of ourselves can rock
just-born babies in our arms, look into the eyes
of the stars, exhale and rest in the arms of love.

reflection questions:
1. Where do you see war and power-hungry ones at work?
2. What might return them to awe?
3. What would it, or does it feel like to exhale and rest in the arms of love?

THE MOTHER OF NIGHT

The mother of night comes to you
when you are alone, curled
like a fawn into yourself—
wondering if anything
you have ever done matters,
if your breath counts—
if anyone understands
the tongue you speak.

She comes to you
when you wonder who will tend
the stone altars by the sea
when you are gone—the ones
you created lifetimes ago
to remember the names
of the peoples who remember you.

The mother of night comes
when you are full of the grief
of the world—when war and hunger
and division seem to be the only language
humans know—and the brokenhearted
wander with boxes of bones
they are still trying to mend.

The mother of night wraps you
in her arms, pulls you into the warm balm
of a darkness so soft you remember
your own beauty. She says you belong
to this fertile dark as much as to the light—
and reminds you that you are filled
with starfields and swallows.
She touches your scars and speaks
the stories of these wounds
even as she heals them.

And when you have forgotten
what you are—when you have forgotten
the ways you are forever woven with all beings—
when you have forgotten that birth
comes from death comes from birth—
she shows you this sacred circle—
and hums the songlines that guide you
along the pathways of dawn,
where whole worlds are revealed
in a single droplet of dew.

reflection questions:
1. What do you think is meant by the Mother of Night?
2. How might you belong to the fertile darkness and also the light?
3. What is the consolation suggested in this poem?

DRINKING STARLIGHT

In December, starlight pours
through the body like wine.
Long nights wrap around us—
a few hours of daylight,
a blink of the sun's eye on the body—
and then back to the down and in.

Here, there is an inner fire that burns—
a stoking that can only happen
when the blaze of summer gives way
to velvet darkness, to the breath of silence,
to the wings of the feathered sky.

All that once flowed up and out
of the trunk into the leaves, now flows
down and into the roots. All that
lives below in the underland is
filled and revitalized. The rivers
under the rivers. The seas under the seas.
The mountains under the mountains.
The heart beneath the heart.

This is where the wanderer goes now.
Here, to the wild, trackless territory.
A place where no map can guide.
Here we find the ancient handprints
of our ancestors on cave walls
reaching through time. Here we find
the paintings of horses running across stone
in the glow of our own inner light.

In this place, the sound of a single tone
is enough to feast on—for all
is spun back to its essence.
In these days we hum a song strung
from the notes between the notes.
We write stories that live between
the lines of our plot line.
We dream with dark matter.
We lean into. Listen into.

In December, the starlight pours
into the body like wine. Drink deeply—
for our very lives depend on it.

reflection questions:
1. How do you experience the darkness and starlight of winter?
2. How can winter help you go deep into your inner life?
3. How and why do our "very lives depend" on the messages of winter?

CHOICE

Push the river
drive the wheel
shoulder the grindstone
command the world
to do your bidding
run off with sacks of gold
brush the shoulders of the gods
become immortal
and then you will be King
of your own world.

A pathway opens
late afternoon light flickers
in tall seeded grasses
twists and turns
a sky full of star scatter
there are others in the meadow
waiting for you
there are others in the sky
calling your name
there is a brilliant arc
around the sun of your life
and wherever you go
you are home.

reflection questions:
1. What are the two ways of being and seeing and acting being contrasted here?
2, When have you had to make a choice between these two?
3. How does nature open the "brilliant arc around the sun of your life?"

HIDE AND SEEK

Did you really think you needed to dig
in the caverns of soul for a few more decades?

Did you really think you needed to embark
on one more excavation of your wounds?

Haven't you been down there with your headlamp
for centuries, chipping away at the walls,

looking for the remains of your own origin story?
Ah, just down this hallway, just through this other

dark passageway, then I'll find the key.
There you are, crawling on your belly, covered in ash—

when a voice calls down to you, saying,
Beloved—this Game is over!

Come out, come out wherever you are!

reflection questions:
1. Have you been "excavating your wounds" for too long?
2. What is meant by "your own origin story?"
3. What kind of game of hide and seek might you play, and with whom?

BEARING WITNESS

Sometimes, all that is needed is to bear witness—
this, the elephants say to me in dreams
as they thunder through the passageways
of my heart, disappearing into a blaze of stars.

On the edge of the sixth mass extinction,
with species vanishing before our eyes,
we'd be a people gone mad
if we did not grieve.

This unmet grief, an elder tells me—
is the root of the root of the collective illness
that got us here. He says tears are medicine
and grief a generous willingness
to look loss in the eye, and let
the cleansing rains of the heart come.

In this way, we do not pass this weight on
in invisible mailbags for the next generation
to carry. In this way, grief doesn't build
and build like sets of waves, until,
at some point down the line—
it simply becomes an unbearable ocean.

We are so hungry when we are fleeing
our grief, when we are doing all we can
to distract ourselves from the heft
of the unread letters of our ancestors.

In my dreams, the elephants stampede in herds—
trumpeting, shaking the earth. See us, they say.
We may not pass this way again.

What if our grief, given as a sacred offering,
is a blessing not a curse?
What if our grief, unhidden,
becomes a kind of communion?
What if our grief is a liberation song
that returns to our innocence?

What if we could simply Bear Witness?

reflection questions:
   1. How might unmet grief be the root of collective illness?
   2. How might grief be a sacred offering, a blessing?
   3. What does bearing witness mean to you, ask of you?

DEEP TIME

Will you plant trees in dirt lots
for generations you will never meet?

Will you re-wild the desecrated spaces
that have forgotten the ways they were
once adorned with necklaces of praise?

Will you go to the sacred springs
to drink the wise waters
that run from glaciers to tongue?

Will you put your ear to the voices
in the layers of canyon stone
that have been unheard for eons?

Will you lay naked by a high-country lake
in the jewel box of paintbrush
and make love to the ancient sun?

Will you dream back the vast canopies
of the rain forest that once burned
when the world had forgotten its true name?

Will you make kin with the bristlecone pine
and taste the blue sap of she who has stood
a thousand years guarding this valley?

Will you reach through deep time
and touch the fingertips of cave dwellers
drawing horses on the walls in ochre?

Will you plant seeds
that will remember you
when you are gone?

reflection questions:
1. How could you honor nature by re-wilding her—and you?
2. How could you reach through "deep time?"
3. Are you willing to plant seeds you may never see growing tall?

FINDING EVE

Are we really still talking about the fall?
Thinking that heavenly kingdoms—
eternities away from *here* and *now*—
are where we are really meant to be?

Bend down to this spring
and taste the waters flowing here.
Let the mists of this October moon
fill the palms of your hand
and open the back door
of the heart chamber.

To know this mammalian love
is unique across this vast universe.
Just ask any mother what awoke in her
when she lifted her newborn to the sky
for the first time. Or a lover, who has merged
the curves of their body with another,
uttering the name of the Divine
again and again.

But once again, we are dissatisfied—
stirring up trouble, dreaming up worlds
based on original deficiency.
For in that mythos we fall away from the One—
dwelling here in the hovels of the forgotten—
praying to be lifted up and away
from all that is mortal and fecund.

I am not sure who this story serves
beyond all the landlords in heaven
getting rich off our monthly penance!
With all that is possible,
why would we keep choosing stories
that have us running from ourselves
towards a distant gleaming city on the horizon?

Why would we choose a story that
makes a hell of a heaven—and
then has us building empires and
armies to prove this is so?

Take a bite of the apple.
There are generations waiting
to feast from the seeds of the fruits
we have been given—these seeds
encoded with the living word.
This is the scripture, the path back.

What is to be remembered—
is that there was never any fall at all.

reflection questions:
1. What do you believe about the Biblical story of Adam and Eve?
2 What evidence do you see that heaven is right here?
3. How could "taking a bite of the apple" be "the path back?"

Pearl Diving

The way, within us, the grit
forms the pearl. You know how this goes.
First the irritation. Something is not right!

And then the way we learn to lay
the opalescent balm—to grow
something new from the seed
of what agitates.

The way the sting can be a medicine.
Or a toxin an intoxicant that reveals the
God inside. Or the heart piercing—
the entry place for a new song.

Bless the grit
that brings forth
your own magic.

Dive into that sweet ocean within
and find the treasure boxes
spilling over with pearls.

reflection questions:
1. Has something new ever emerged for you from an inner irritation?
2. How or when can a sting prove to be a medicine?
3. Are you willing to dive deep to find a treasure box of pearls?

MIND

The divine does not come to us through the mind.
Though the mind is itself, divine.

Mind is like an old friend who chatters too much—
and tells you stories you've heard a thousand times before.

When we see this, we can lean back and enjoy
the tall tales. And at some point, when the noise

is just too much—we can ask for the check,
head home and fall into the arms of silence.

reflection questions:
1. How do you feel about the first stanza?
2. Is your mind like the old friend in this poem?
3. How do you "fall into the arms of silence?"

THREE: **on the riverbank**

OASIS

How long will you pack
the camel of your soul
with the bags of your past—
thinking you still need
all of those precious memories?

There is a wide and wise desert ahead.
There are vast galaxies and fertile oases
to see. With all that weight
you won't make it over the first dune!

Strip yourself to bare essentials.
Then the desert will welcome you
into her arms. And the camel
will stand a chance of making it
beyond these blowing sands
to the jewel of the sea.

reflection questions:
1. What kinds of baggage do you carry from your past?
2. What would it be like to "strip to the bare essentials?"
3. How could such "lightness" get you through "the desert of life?"

QUANTUM ENTANGLEMENT

I convinced you long ago of my sovereignty.
That seemed so important then. To prove
I could stand alone, unique, untangled.

But this was all a game of hide and seek.
Particle and wave. For the truth is I revel
in the ways your quanta dance with mine—

this celestial tango right here and now—
our feet on the earth. And you and I, this web
that weaves and unweaves itself with no weaver.

reflection questions:
1. In a primary relationship of yours, is it important to "prove your sovereignty?"
2. How is that a game of hide and seek?
3. In what ways are our close relationships a "celestial tango?"

CANYONLANDS

Today I come to the well of an ancient desert—
a place yes, but more of a reunion—
the way you feel when meeting an elder
who has whispered to you all of your life.

Here, the rock is awash with spiral
and wave, with curve and spire.
Here, inland seas have come and gone,
leaving us this Library of Beauty.

Here, the silence is so deep
it reminds us of our first mother—
the one whose arms we have never left.

And rounding the bend to another canyon
amongst canyons, we see this reflection
of our own mystery—the impossibility
of this moment—how we have come
to stand here, in this eon, in this sliver of time
as the thunder clouds rumble on the horizon,
as the lightning flashes over spines of juniper.

And we so small and full of earnest prayer,
we bow down and ask to enter.
For there are guardians here—
ones who weave the mythos of the ages,
ones who hear us when all seems lost.

For we have played hide and seek
here before, in these canyons of time—
in this endless labyrinth of being,
in these cathedrals of swallows and wind.

This is the holy of holies—
where moonflowers bloom from red soil
where hummingbirds whir through golden grottos
where rainbows arc over honeycombs of stone.

If all of humanity stood under a starfield like this
for just one breath, we couldn't help but love each other.

If all of humanity stood under a starfield like this
we couldn't help but know exactly how we belong.

reflection questions:
1. Have you been to a place in nature you might call a Library of Beauty?
2. Do holy lands speak to you of "the impossibility of this moment?"
3. How could the awe expressed in this poem help us to love each other?

SEEDS

Darling, lay here with me awhile—
let the stories of our skins sink into
each other—so that we speak not only
of the love song between us,
but listen too for the stories
in the hearts of our ancestors.

You take me to the land of red soil
and green corn, the back roads
lined with people who are kind
because they come from the earth
and know what they belong to.

How we laugh with the men
at the roadside stand as they fill paper bags
with fresh red chiles whose seeds
have lived in their family for generations.
And all the while, you beside me,
and a voice singing out through the car radio
that says, *even now in this age of cruelty
there are flowers of beauty that will save us.*

We will save us, as we reach for sweet waters—
give thanks because we know
that each drop is scarce—that the rivers
rarely return to the sea anymore,
that the glistening serpentine Rio Grande
is so very low this year of fire and drought,
of plague and war. This, a year that could drive
all hope underground and leave us
with nothing to eat but despair.

But in the midst of this: miracles.
The simple kind. The kind that can feed
the peoples, turn water into wine,
multiply loaves of bread

How a mother's body knows just how
to make the milk to grow a baby,
the unique remedy required. And a seed,
when you put it in your mouth,
will grow fruit in the soils of your garden
with just the particular codes
of nourishment for the temple of *your* body.

When we return to the roots of our belonging,
all is given. For this is the medicine
that transforms the people made of bitter
into the people made of honey.

And as we drive through the last
of the sunset light, as we stop
to gather wild sage off the highway,
I see that it is this returning to the simple,
to the extraordinary ordinary,
that allows the heart to become
a hive full of golden nectar.

reflection questions:
  1. In this poem about an intimate relationship, how does the poet listen to the song of our
     ancestors?
  2. What are some "flowers of beauty" that could save us?
  3. Where and how could you find the seeds and roots of your belonging?

SOLAR RETURN

Every year, the sun comes around again
to kiss the moment we were born.
And every year, the cycles come faster—
the orbit of life somehow speeding up
as seasons flow one into the other—
becoming a river of light, a holy trembling.

Here, our unique shape—we the one
who came with *this* name, *this* particular face,
this soul song that moves through us
in a swelling symphony—
sometimes wild and brazen,
other times, soft and intricate
like songbirds at dusk.

After many decades, the sword
of the spirit given to the tempering
fires again and again—so that we emerge
strong and flexible. Perhaps here
we remember the dignity of humility—
of knowing we are both ash and eternal flame—
nothing and everything. A miracle.

And so today you hear your name on the wind—
that, which is the name of every child
who belongs to this wild earth. You feel
what it is to be birthed in this holy hour,
under the influence of this phase of the moon—
when the ancestors circled round
to welcome you to this circle of being.
And from the moment of your crowning,
to ride the tides and currents of this life.
To know beauty as the path—
and joy as a choice.

Every year, the sun comes around again
and strikes the bell of our original impulse
to tumble into time, into a body.
And in this solar return is the call
to renew your vows to Wonder
and marry this world once more.

reflection questions:
 1. Do birthdays help you remember the miracle of your life?
 2. What is meant by "the dignity of humility?"
 3. Can you view your birthday as "the call to renew your vows to wonder?"

GOD IS THE CRACK

Deep in the crack between towering sandstone
the tree of eternity blooms—this wise juniper
with spiraled trunk and serpentine roots.

She is older than memory –and the wings
of her branches drop silver berries into high desert soils—
an act of divine faith to put seeds down here.

Yes, God is the crack—God is the place life emerges—
disruptive and outrageous. Not the ordered heavens
where all hums along in temperature-controlled glory.

But this storm, this rumble that trembles our bones,
this blaze of lightning, this precious rain on our upturned faces,
leaving pools in hollows of lichen-streaked rock.

God is the crack. The way the down of the milkweed
splits the husk, the way the egg shatters into furry body
and untried wings. God is the way the rainbow

of mushrooms explodes out of earth after storm—
this living neural web that transforms the forest.
God is this life that depends on rupture—

thrives in places where edges meet. And yet,
we seek the comfort of the familiar eddies—
as if this would save us from being part of *everything*—

as if this would save us from the torrent of time
carving us into new shapes we have never been before.
God is the crack. It is the place where the gold lettering

of your soul speaks its truth—where the dandelion
defies the concrete—and the mustard seed turns
an abandoned lot into a parable that would feed the world.

reflection questions:
  1. Can you see God in "the place life emerges—disruptive and outrageous?"
  2. Where in nature do you see life as a miracle?
  3. What does the mustard seed turning the lot into a parable mean to you?

WILD PLUMS

It's erotic—my hands sifting through
plum flesh for pits—the purple skins,
the golden juice like a fine wine—
this bowl overflowing. But wait,
there is more to this story.

There is the moment when we stood
in the September dusk in the storm light—
women laughing in awe at the choreography
of harvest moon and the late summer wind
blowing through branches so laden with plums,
they fall off by the dozens into our palms.

Gathering to harvest the way peoples
have always gathered. Each to make
our own version of plum jam—
the alchemy of this particular summer,
where grief and beauty have been lovers,
where we have all lost someone—
where we all have sung river songs
by the river and laid our bare bodies
on rocks in the sun, finding the places
where our mythologies weave—
where we dream not only for ourselves
but for each other.

This is the taste of a summer
that will be remembered in mid-winter—
carried in the essence of these plums.
Bright stars and purple asters.
Owl song and deer rustle. This moment
of equal day and night, just before the sun
slants south to become the thin light of winter.

But wait, I am here, standing in the kitchen
my hands plunged into a bowl of pulp,
plums boiling on the stove
thinking of all the ways we make love
with life, all the ways we are given
to commune with the fruits of the world—
so freely given. So freely given.

reflection questions:
1. What do wild plums symbolize for you in this poem?
2. Do you remember a summer when "grief and beauty have been lovers?"
3. For you, what are "all the ways we make love with life?"

CROSSROADS

We stand under a river of stars
at the edge of one galaxy amidst billions—
for just this minute. Tonight,
Jupiter rises with the moon,
glowing blue against the black sky.
Somehow it echoes the way I feel,
finding myself here with you,
in the land of our ancestors.

I feel our lineages talking—
working things out, having a good cry,
telling stories over the fire that burns
at the center of the Milky Way.

And through the heat of our palms
I know there are eons and landscapes
and old songs speaking with each other—
so that I feel the mystery of you
pouring into the mystery of me.

Perhaps this is how the stars feel
when they meet in the vastness of space—
a gratitude. Perhaps they too find
a third language between them.
This is how bodies find each other
in the night—how we trace the maps
of scars and springs that live
in the wild territory of the heart.

And this meadow, encircled by aspen,
is like a dream I have had over and over
for centuries and finally remember.
For I am here with you in this crossroads
of time and space—remembering
all the roads and roses, the blood
and harvests it took to arrive here—
in the arms of this diamond night,
for just this minute.

reflection questions:
  1. Have you felt the ancientness of your relationship with another?
  2. How might feeling the mystery of being here be a crossroads?
  3. How might the awe of a crossroads moment open new possibilities?

UNDERLAND

All of our life we are taught
to spread our wings like Icarus—
to fly as high as we can towards the sun.
Such is the way of a world
full of transcendent gods.

The other day I climbed a thousand-year-old
bristlecone pine, felt my small body nested
in her wise coiling roots
pushing up from hard earth,
a labyrinth within the mountainside.

We yearn endlessly for the infinite above us
when we are tap dancing on the cathedral
of the infinite just beneath our feet.

How the underland teems
with conversations we forget to listen to.
Rivers of magma,
electric networks of mycelium,
flowing dark aquifers.
All of these voices speaking.

What is it that your heart wants?
This is the question that sings from beneath.
Beyond the bright lights of the upper world.
Beyond the habit of endless activity.
What is it that your heart really wants?

And what is it to grow the tree of our souls
with equal attention to the roots as to the branches?

reflection questions:
  1. In what way do we live in "a world full of transcendent gods?"
  2. When have you experienced "the cathedral of the infinite...beneath our feet?"
  3. What does your heart really want?

LOST CANYON
Needles District, Utah

We are so resistant to veering off the known path—
one unfamiliar turn and we no longer know who or what we are.

But in the folds of this canyon, being lost has a different meaning.
Here, we have lost the way we have needed to lose.

Here we wander beyond human imprint, following game trails
and coyote print, to find pools of rainwater—

where the face behind our own face is reflected back
in silver flashing mirrors. Here, we bend down to touch streamflow

and sing to every rare drop of water that is a holy well
for bee and dragonfly. We stroke smooth curves of golden sandstone,

step beyond the monotony of linear time—dislodge the sense
of the human self as the center of everything.

And as the fullness of the October moon rises over pyramids
of slickrock, the deep hum of the universe ripples through

this silence in shades of rose and umber. And in this moment,
we don't recognize our selves anymore—as we unwind

from all that has bound us to the wound we were born with.
For here, getting lost has meant losing what is necessary to be found.

reflection questions:
1. Do you resist veering off the known path and feeling lost?
2. When and where has nature changed your view of yourself?
3. When has "getting lost" helped you find something about yourself?

THE LIGHTNING TREE

Mid-summer heat—the air electric with the coming storm.
And when the sky explodes open with lightning—
I run into the street to see what remains.

There on the corner is a century-old spruce—
body shattered into a thousand points of light,
the air singing with the scent of sap and ozone.

Some clearing has happened. Some reckoning.
Some transmission from heaven to earth,
like an oracle that ignites after the message is given.

I pick up branches, bark, fragments of trunk—
sap pouring into my hands. And in that scent
I recognize how I too know the power of the lightning,

my life having been cracked open again and again.
So many deaths and births will tumble through us—
so many lifetimes in this lifetime. And so now

there is this next moment along the blooming path
of being. And now, the crystalline air
after the hard rain. And now, this shining sky.

And now, three gold finches fluttering amidst the leaves
and petals, feeding on scattered seeds—
carrying away tiny branches for new nests.

reflection questions:
1. When has your life been cracked open like a tree struck by lightning?
2. What kinds of deaths and rebirths have you experienced in this lifetime?
3. What kinds of deaths and rebirths happen every moment in nature?

FOUR: **surrendering to the flow**

BURNING THE MAPS

Who is captaining this ship?
you ask, when the sails flag
and the boat lists without direction.

Who is minding the store?
you demand, when all of life seems
a random assortment of events—
the elements fierce and unresponsive.

Who is directing the symphony?
you call, when the cymbals of your heart
crash and your world is full
of clanging dissonance.

What does it all mean? you say,
when destiny lays a card before you
that you never imagined
you'd ever have to play.

And you wonder to yourself:
Perhaps I did not receive the necessary maps
for this kind of impenetrable terrain.
Perhaps I did not read the fine print
of my soul contract before I slid down
the ladders in the sky to meet this world
of shadows and light. For surely,
I would not have agreed to all of this!

You pull out your file folders and old journals
looking for the thread of your destiny.
You look at your Life under a microscope—
through one philosophical lens and then another.
You get out the maps—
dozens and dozens of maps!

A thousand myths we have lived—
and in all of them, we are the hero.
Oh, the sheer thrill and exhaustion of
the seeking, of the vanquishing!

And yet here is the Beloved at your table,
brandishing matches, whispering—
Burn all the maps—every last one of them!
And you laugh, astonished—and set it all ablaze.
Watching as the hero of you turns to ash.

And now you are naked in trackless territory—
untethered from any quest
that would distract you from the truth
of what your soul is here to be.

reflection questions:
1. Have you been a seeker in the inner world?
2. Do you wonder who is in charge and where the maps are?
3. What do you imagine you would feel or do if you set the maps ablaze?

KIN

Last night we sat together in the silence—
all circled around a central flame—
where the faces of those
who have crossed over appeared
in a stream of eyes, of essence—
reminding us that they are still
a part of this world's conversation.

So many beings are gathering around
this planet's council fire, to midwife
the unraveling, to tend the spirit
of the new world quickening inside us all.
And yet birth is never guaranteed.

There is a delicacy to what is embryonic—
and these are fierce times.
For we know War is on the minds
of so many who only know the allure
of adrenaline and power without love.

I still drop to my knees before a redwood
and ask why humanity turn towards
the drumbeat of this dark machine
again and again—while the stars
on the sea show us another path.
Why do we turn again to wars
we have already fought and lost?
Why do we feel a need to burn it
down to feel the heat?

And yet within us,
there is a memory dreamed with others—
in the middle of the night or in those moments
of silence around a flame—a memory
of a different kind of eternal return—
where rivers flow all the way to the ocean
where we grow food in rich loamy soils—
where we know there is enough.

This, not some distant past revived—
nor a distant utopia—but a knowing
of what is already within us—
a pathway to a prayer we recognize—
some center place of kinship.
That is what I bow to in these times—
this eternal return, this flame.

reflection questions:
1. Have you been to a fire ceremony where you remembered those on the other side?
2. Why do you think so many are drawn to war?
3. What experiences bring back the memory of our kinship to each other?

ORIGINAL SUFFICIENCY

For a moment you let yourself
receive the fulfillment of this holy moment.
For a moment the bluebells and the birdsong
and the lapping of the lake are enough.

But then, what is missing moves in you
like a strange fish swimming in the depths
of the most exquisite pool—
a golden carp hiding in the shadows.

And in that moment, you wonder
if you are in the wrong time or place—
or if there is simply a better somewhere to be.

It's a kind of existential fear
of not getting it right that has you
doubt and second guess—
until you are a ball of knots
rather than a chalice of fulfillment.

You are the hungry fish
that won't let yourself taste the feast of now
because you are so preoccupied
with the banquet down the road.
The somewhere *else* of perfection!
From here, you can't possibly
be available for divine union!

But then one day, the fish surfaces
and reveals its true nature—and you gaze
mesmerized into each other's eyes—
endless reflections of golden light.

And in this reflection, you see
there was never anything missing—
and that fulfillment is yours
for the receiving. You only need
to fully pick up the chalice and drink—
you only need to see again
that you are born of original sufficiency.

reflection questions:
1. What kind of moments make you feel the present moment isn't enough?
2. What is the nature of the "hungry fish" who thinks you aren't enough?
3. What changes for you when you believe you were born of "original sufficiency?"

WHAT SHAPES US

When the undersea volcano exploded—
we shuddered at the way the top
of the caldera blew, the way the great wave
rippled out across the globe—the way
ash rained down, blackening the land.

Yes—devastating for human lives,
for the structures we've created,
for the stability we want.
And yet, these magma rivers
welling up from the molten core
are what we are made of—
this fire at the center of stars,
this eros at the heart of living.

And it is the ferocity of this life force
that we run from—what we build fortresses
to protect against and religions to tame.
But we have come to remember
our kinship with the undomesticated wild—
with jungle root and river vein,
with stampede of bison and tangle
of mangrove. With bottomless lake
and blooming waterfall.

So, gather your body of light.
Dream yourself wilder and wilder
Until you know the face
of the world as your own.

reflection questions:
1. How is "this fire at the center of stars/this eros at the heart of living" what we are made of?
2. Where do you see "the undomesticated wild?"
3. How could you "dream yourself wilder and wilder," and what might the result be?

MUSTANG

He came in the night, no humans to witness.
Just the stars and the circle of mares, breathing deep
while he emerged—first soft hooves, then too-long legs,
then creamy head with the swirl on his brow
where Epona must have kissed him.

For he was born from the wild,
an undomesticated foal whose mother
galloped wild in a herd of mustang,
just before the roundup, his father unknown.

How he stood up on those untried legs
and fell down again into a deep sleep,
over and over he moved between worlds
deciding where he would stay. He lay his head
in our laps, as he dreamed himself deeper
into springtime and a broad back.

reflection questions:
1. If Epona, a Celtic goddess associated with horses and fertility, kissed the Mustang, what
   does the swirl on his head feel like to you?
2. What feelings about birth lie within this poem?
3. Do you think, as we're being born, we decide between worlds?

SONG OF THE ANCESTORS
for Elder Malidome Some

Tonight the ancestors circle close—
and candles flicker between worlds
where souls pass to and fro.

I have heard them coming and going—
murmuring prayers, humming songs
that come from the center of the earth.

There are those who tend the portals
through time. There are those who dwell
in the canyons, caves, and lakes who sing
the whole world into being
again and again.

There are those who hold the drumbeat
through the rise and fall of empire
and sit at the loom at the center
of the universe to weave the next story.

Tonight the ancestors circle close—
and we who have forgotten how
to tend the holy are being asked to remember.

To clear the patterns that have twisted
the essence of our lineage.
To make amends.
To bring honey and balm to the places
in ourselves that have carried
wounds and atrocities.
To call down the blessings of the line
that reimagines itself through our living.

Some say all the pains of the world,
all the great imbalances of our time,
come from the restlessness
of the unrecognized ancestors.
And some say that all the beauty
of the world comes from the visions
of the descendants, calling us forth.

For we too will pass in and out
of bodies—through the hallways of time.
We will be called upon by our grandchildren's
grandchildren—to illuminate the way awhile
with the lantern the size of the moon.
We will be asked about the magic of old—
that most ordinary magic
of seasons and light and seeds.

Tonight, the ancestors' circle closes
and our hearth fires speak in their tongue.
Lay the table with marigold and pomegranate,
with scarlet leaves and gourds. For together
we are already dreaming the next year's arc.
Together, we are already dreaming
 the story to come.

reflection questions:
 1. How does a ceremonial space enable us to bring the ancestors close?
 2. How do the ancestors remind us "how to tend the holy?"
 3. What kind of ancestor do you want to be for your descendants?

VOWS

Vows are not unchanging—
not like locks in a door
that only open with a single key—
not untouchable and eternal.

A vow is like the promise
of monsoon rain. It is a living
contract between our hearts
and the Great Heart of the World.

The way any two intimates
must continue to find new ways
to tend the spring of their love
as we age and transform
before each other's eyes.

New vows come—
because the old ones
would bind us to pathways
that are no longer.

These days, my vows
are more about leaning back in the boat
and letting the current take me
all the way to the edges of the galaxy and back—
carrying baskets of starlight to pass
to the generations to come.

Yes, now the vows are less about destination
and more about the holy moment
that is always opening within us.
The way the cranes fill the sky
when I am having a conversation
with my own heart. Or the way
we hold each other in the night
around the council fires.

To cultivate a garden of joy.
To keep weaving the tapestry
of the new story, even as the old
one unravels. To marvel at the Mystery
that won't be solved like a puzzle.

To share the basket of starlight
with the great grandchildren
I do not yet know.
This is my vow.

reflection questions:
   1. Do you find your vows have changed?
   2. What are your current vows?
   3. How might you "share the baskets of starlight" with great-great-grandchildren you don't
      yet know?

GOLDEN FEATHER

I saw you in the sky yesterday—your wings
spread out to the edges of eternity.
It was as if you had forgotten
your outworn ways—and waves of joy
shimmered in the late light on your feathers.

But then, as I watched, you seemed to reach
the edge of an invisible horizon—the boundary
of familiar territory. Some tether pulled you back—
as if some great distraction caught all your attention.

You wobbled in your flight—looked down,
and in that looking, plummeted to the ground
where you began to peck at the same square
of terrain you've pecked at for centuries—
pecking at all those old places that hurt.
There are a thousand holes
in that well-trodden ground!

Perhaps there comes a time to leave it all alone—
to unhook from those tethers of the mind
and send the mad logician home.
No more need to try so hard to solve
the paradox of being a single dancing body
in a World Soul—or the body of the world
dancing as a single soul.
It is only the crucible of humanness.

I saw you in the sky yesterday—
your wings spread out to the edges of eternity.
And now I will bring you the golden feather
that dropped from your wing.
I will remind you not to look back.

reflection questions:
    1. Do you try hard to figure out in your mind what life is all about?
    2. When can you choose to let it all go?
    3. What would happen if you flew above the old hurtful problems and didn't look back?

BOWL OF LIGHT
for Mary Wilder

When cancer first came to my young body—
as it had come to my mother, grandmother
and great grandmother, I thought I was
to take on the wounds of the lineage.
To solve the glitch.
To go into the minefields,
searching under every rock
for the key to our liberation.

It was then that an ancestor came to me—
an old one from eight generations back
before the Great Forgetting. She said—
not so long ago in your ancestral lands
the women tended the wells—holy openings
where the waters fill the veins of the earth.

But then that contract was broken—
by those who forgot what they belong to.
The land was laid to waste, the springs
dried up—and our connection to the old way
was buried under church stones and liturgy.

She said, it is the dis-ease of broken-heartedness
that has run so deep through the line of women—
that at times they have not known how to go on.

And what she pointed to then was not the weight
of the crushing wounds, or the burden of despair—
but the unstoppable light blazing through
all the places that had been pierced.

Yes, it was the eros that had survived
and flourished—a geyser of love blasting
through the rock and steel of loss,
showing us how to remake ourselves
in our own sacred image.

My ancestor came close to me then—
and in her hands was a wide vessel brimming
with this nectar of light for me to drink—
and for me to pass on.

She showed me the way reciprocity works—
how when we tend the earth, the earth tends us.

And as I drank this bowl of light,
I felt the stones dislodge
from those ancient springs
so the waters could run
clear and wild once again.

reflection questions:
1. Has an ancestor ever come to you with wisdom?
2. How could the dis-ease of broken-heartedness and broken contracts affect our health?
3. How might love and light pierce our wounds and heal ancestral patterns?

DIVING FOR PEARLS

Perhaps we chose to blindfold ourselves—
the way when we came to this world
we drank from the River of Lethe to forget
what our souls knew of that other place.

Perhaps we took on the chosen wound—
the perfect opening in the ribs
where the sword of the world
would touch us with its fire—
to open us to the vulnerability
at the center of our own being.

Perhaps we decided to play
the Sacred Fool in our own story—
to meet ourselves at the crossroads
in the form of the crone and point
the way down a road less taken.

Perhaps we chose to forget who we are
so we could swim in the sea of mystery,
dive for pearls of meaning,
string them together
to make the story of our life.

And perhaps, in moments,
we let the blindfold slip, so the illusion
no longer holds—the spirit blazing
through the emptiness of us—
so we see how it is the nature of our soul
to slip inside these different skins,
dive into this festival of being—
and gather pearls of remembrance,
to bring back to the hearth
of our own eternal fire.

reflection questions:
1. Do you believe we chose to blindfold ourselves to who we truly are?
2. How do you dive for pearls of meaning?
3. What kinds of "pearls of remembrance" have you gathered?

HARVEST

Standing in a trembling grove of aspen,
tasting the fire in their release—
I see all the moments in my journey
as shimmering leaves
on the Tree of Life.

And I see how all of these moments—
even the ones I have prayed
could stay—will turn to gold,
speak their story, and fall
back into this black earth.

How I never could have never imagined
this face of mine after five decades—
the unique shape of this life of mine,
the particular harvest baskets I carry
full of the seeded grasses of childhood,
the plums of love, the late summer
blackberries of longing, the boughs
of elderhood that beckon to me now.

We are travelers through a life
that rewrites itself again and again,
season after season, so we become
unrecognizable even to ourselves.

And as time passes, we become more
intimate with all that is transitory—
resting into the unknowable,
all the urgent questions falling away,
become chaff for the next growing season.

So now there is the bliss that arises
from this particular quality of light—
the scent of these leaves, the silver crescent
of moon in violet sky, the imprint
of all we love and all that loves us.

As evening comes, starlings murmurate—
spectacular oracles speaking
in the language of wings and wind.
And I feel the autumn weaving
its magic again on the loom of my being
for another round of seasons—

And this blessed weight
of my harvest baskets
filling and emptying
and filling once again.

reflection questions:
1. How has your life become unrecognizable?
2. When can you "rest in the unknowable?"
3. How does Autumn remind you of both the beauty and impermanence of
   our life's harvests?

FIVE: **where the river meets the sea**

QUICKENING

God kissed me in the night—
and then came a quickening,
as if tulips burst through
the dark soils of me.
It was so simple, such a delight—
it brought sweet laughter for all
the pain I think I've endured.

The soul doesn't see it this way!
It's all about the awakening—
what will remind the seed
that it has other places to go!
That it has a flower to become.
And then what reminds the flower
in time to fall back to earth—
to go to seed.

Perhaps all of our lifetimes
we have been seeking immortality
when we have been immortal all along!
This body, sweet mercy, this temple
that allows the soul to shape-shift
into a thousand forms of creation.
This is God's delight.

We run from our own horizon
because we think it is the end of "us"!
And it is!

And then we—
And the horizon
move on.

reflection questions:
    1. What might be meant by "God kissed me?"
    2. How do you run from death?
    3. Do you believe your soul is immortal?

KAIROS

i.
Shapeshifting is as old as time itself.
It's what life does. It's what life is.
And we, these vessels—becoming
fur and fin and claw,
mycelial in our intelligence
and yet still insisting
on our separateness—
as if this would counter impermanence—
from falling into the cauldron of Love
where we are so thoroughly stewed.

ii.
How immortality struck a bargain
with the world—saying,
Oh holy One, please let me be mortal awhile.
And yet, we've forgotten to rest, to daydream—
to gaze at a waterfall all afternoon—
we have forgotten to drink from the well of Kairos.

iii.
How the long tide of the whale
and the ebb and flow of the sea
teach me that everything is Breath.

How the body is mostly empty space—
fields of waving poppies, spring winds
and bird wings—all made of dark matter.

iv.
Goddess of fractal fields, of effulgent
blooming and returning.
God of lightning who blazes with seed.
Who is the great Devourer of Time?

How long does it take for the Guardian
of the Yuga to Blink? And in that gap
when the eye is closed—how is it
that all of creation dissolves into Radiant Void?

v.

Just outside of Bolinas, I drive
the sinuous road, following the curve
of the land. Here a lagoon
where dozens of sea lion roll up
on fingerlets of sand in late light, here—
oyster shells line the shores of the bay.

I gather tiny yellow flowers
I don't know the names of,
growing between grass blades,
miracles no one ever sees.
I put them in a vase, next to
the ocean-washed jade stones
and the half-broken spirals of mollusks.

I make an altar to this Whorl
that grows from the center of me,
through the center of you,
through the center of a redwood
to the milky way. This whorl
of our essence that is our fingerprint,
our map, our eternal return.

reflection questions:
1. How is shapeshifting "what life is?"
2. How might you "drink from the well of Kairos"?
3. As the poet makes an altar to "this whorl of our essence," to what is she returning?

TRINITY
For David 1971-2021

We walk barefoot over warm earth—
you with a walking staff, leaning into me
for balance. Through the just plowed fields,
under the old fence, across the low sway
of stream trickling because drought
has been on the land for years now.
What it is to love and pray in these times
the old ones have sung about,
have prophesied, for centuries.

And now, these days are *here*, and we are here.
And as we stand in the burnished summer fields
of waist-high golden grass and chicory,
as we speak of the presence of illness
in both of our bodies, of what it is to live
with the ally of death on our shoulders—
of how we feel divine life force pulsing
through every cell of our beings—
first one white-tailed kite,[1] then another,
and then a third converge above us.

---

1. *kites are a kind of raptor, related to hawks*

They swoop and dive and circle
in this dance of three—like you and me
and the holy spirit—and a doorway
between worlds opens. And their wings
catch the light as they carve the air.
And their cries seem to say to us—
there is no death, there is no death—
there is only this miraculous arrival
here in the center, here in the temple of Now.

And I know that, no matter where
our destinies take us, no matter how long
each of us has in these bodies—
this communion is eternal—
and we will always find each other
in the doorway where the three white kites fly—
our feet in the soft dust,
our faces lifted to sky.

reflection questions:
1. Do you have a friend with whom you've felt a holy communion?
2. What do you think is meant by "the doorway where the kites fly?"
3. What do you believe about "there is no death...only this miraculous arrival...in the temple of now?"

THE KING TIDES

Every year the King Tides come
long and strong against the coastlines—
the full spring moon pushing behind
towering swells and sheets of spray.

Today, something draws me close—
closer than is safe. Something in me wants
to take the waves inside me—to be filled
with the sheer open roar of white noise.

There are angels who fly along the arcs
of these waves—the shimmer of heaven
in the iridescent spray—some lust for shoreline—
the union of water and land, mortal and immortal.

Something in the sheer pounding force
reminds me there are far greater forces at work
than my small mind. How, like hermit crabs—
we must leave one home for another—
and we, so vulnerable in between.

And so today I turn to the King Tides
and say yes, take all the old versions
of me back to the sea—for I am ready
for this new shape of myself—for this body

that ripens with the moon and blooms
with April's first calla lilies. This one who
knows how to shapeshift again—
and ride the currents to the waiting shore.

reflection questions:
1. Have you felt the "lust for the union of water and land, mortal and immortal?"
2. How does the ocean remind you of greater forces at work?
3. Are you ready to surrender old versions of yourself?

ALCHEMY

Because you've been down and in
the cauldron of transformation—
deep in the fertile darkness
where the underground waters flow—
and you feel you've been here for an eternity,

you've met your demons and angels.
You've unspun spells and curses—
and unraveled the beliefs that kept you
wedded to the past. You've spit out
the bitter poison of your own resentments.
The holy waters of forgiveness
have soothed the raw places in your soul.

And now, you say to the Beloved—
now you are ready for the next chapter—
to arrive back into the upper world
bearing these hard-earned gifts.

You come to the gates, eager.
And yet still, the Beloved turns you back.
No darling, it's not yet time.
Stay in this alchemical vessel.
The good part is just beginning!

You put your ear to the ground.
press your belly against the earth's belly—
you, who are the cocoon whose
butterfly cannot be rushed.
And you realize it's the very attachment
to living in the shiny, busy world that you
are being asked to release.

For it is not the old one of you who rises,
oh Lazarus. It is the one of you who is
much older than that. This one remembers
the first instructions written in our bones.

This one of you lights a sea of candles—
not because you are afraid of the dark,
but because you have finally seen

that this is not a place simply to endure—
but a sanctuary where you remember
how to sing each of the 10,000 names
of the Holy One.

reflection questions:
1. Have you spent time in the "cauldron of transformation?"
2. Do you wish for rewards in this "shiny, busy world?"
3. Can you see this world as a sanctuary of remembrance?

BONES OF BELONGING

You've been in this love affair for quite some time.
But still, you don't trust God won't walk out the back door
or trade you out for another lover when your shine wears off!

How many times do you need to hear I love you
before you believe it? How many times do you need to feel
the press of flesh against yours to know you are wanted?

How many times are you going to call God an unfaithful lout
when you are wandering along through the lonely moors
or trudging through thick mud in the jungle—feeling abandoned?

Listen, the Beloved says, I made a vow to you an eternity ago
and I've been shouting it from every mountain top ever since.
But you have put your hands over your ears—and cried out—
I can't find you anywhere!

It is as if you have hidden the Beloved in your blindspot
and believed the myth of your own exile.
But now the Beloved sneaks up behind you
and pulls you into an embrace that is bigger than all that.

Now the Beloved says—breathe and feel the bones
of your true belonging. Let the lodestones you thought
you had to carry to pay some ancient debt—simply fall away.

And you look up into the shining eyes of the One
who has always claimed you and say, I see now—
you made your vow and I've been hedging my bets

You look up into the shining eyes of the Beloved
and realize you have tried to bargain for safety
when all along your heart has longed to ring out
with its unfettered devotion.

You look into the shining eyes of the Beloved and say,
Alright then. I'm all in.

And the keys in the lock turn—and the doors
to beauty open and the morning sings a ballad
for star-crossed lovers finally found.

reflection questions:
1. Do you believe "the One" loves you?
2. Do you ever hedge your bets with a lover or with the One?
3. What might happen if you said, "Alright then. I'm all in...?"

ACROSS THE THRESHOLD

What if death were not a failure
but the bright blossom of our green age—
not annihilation but miracle?

What if death is not a cutting but a rooting—
not a cessation but an engagement to a Lover
who will lead you to the River of Forgetting
so you can take your next Breath of Remembering?

What if death is not a failure, but a miracle—
not a nightmare, but a gallop on a silver horse
through the doorways of Twilight?

What if, in our dying, we become
the imaginal cells of a metamorphic universe
that is always turning into a butterfly?

What if we simply become rhizomes
in the Great Fields of Calla Lilies—
gramophones of the Universe playing

all the soul songs human beings ever sang
as we walked along the shorelines
of thousands of lifetimes.

What if we are simply going over
the edge of a rushing falls to the
cool pools beneath, where carp
swim with our great-great-
grandchildren—who are just
preparing to dive into a body.

reflection questions:
1. Do you feel death can be seen as a miracle?
2. How might we turn into imaginal cells?
3. What positive images of death can you imagine?

RIVER OF AWE

When they ask where you have been,
say you have been swimming in the River of Awe again—
dropping skins to arrive here,
to be bathed and reborn in this starlit current.

Some of the most difficult work we will do in our lives—
is to retrieve joy from the clutches of bitterness.

There is a choice along the path—
the many crossroads. Will the crucible of living
soften you, or simply thicken the armor?

In a recurring childhood dream—
I stand at the edge of the sea—
watching a mountain of a wave
surging towards me. In that moment,
I know just how to turn my body inside out
to create an opalescent shell.
So that when the wave crashes,
I tumble unharmed in the wild foam.

A teacher says to me, perhaps it is time to let go of that dream—
for now you know you are the sea itself.

When the fierce visitor of dis-ease or loss has come
into your body, into your own mind-heart—you are asked
to learn how to receive the teachings and let the teacher go.
It is only the raft to the other side of midnight.

A revelation—to see that your story
is not as personal as it all seems.
That the gods are not out to get you.
Nor are they here to save you.

Go to the River of Awe and let the waters
clear the pain of the small self. You may feel
the disorientation of this—of unhooking
from the familiar habit of you. And yet
there you are emerging—the light
streaming off your skin.

You were given this Oracle long ago.
There is an Intimacy with life you are offered.
It requires everything of you.
Even the surrender of the story of the life
you thought was yours to live.
Even the opening to the story of a life
that would bring nectar and miracles—
and set your heart on fire.

reflection questions:
  1. Does the suffering in your life ever feel personal?
  2. What does the "River of Awe" represent to you?
  3. What might happen if you relinquished old bitter stories about your life?

SONG TO THE BELOVED

Broken open, I come to you—
my belly stretched out onto the earth
not in supplication, but in pleasure.

I want you to touch every part of me.
This is how the radiant presence
makes love to us.

My heart spills calla lilies
and hummingbird feathers
and the ache for union.

This eros was the seed the divine
planted in us from the beginning
so we would always remember
to follow the path to the temple.

So no matter how lost or distracted
we got along the way, we would
pick up the diamonds of our own souls
and bring them back to you.

So that, in that great shining communion,
we would dissolve again into the Ecstatic Hum.

reflection questions:
    1. How might you know if the Source or Beloved is touching every part of you?
    2. What does Eros mean to you and how might it keep you on the path?
    3. What do you imagine or feel from the words "Ecstatic Hum?"

THE SILENCE OF THE WORLD

We call out to the world and long
for its reply—a natural impulse to listen
for messages on the wind.

We throw a stone into the lake and wait—
wondering if our prayer has been received—
if *we* are received. And yet the whole of life
reveals itself in relation to the way we listen.

In a dream, the world spoke to me—saying:
remember the times you thought
your prayer was not heard?
We were speaking to you all along.

Every wave washing over your feet.
Every breeze against your face.
Every monarch wing in flight.
When you call out, this diamond light
is the reply. The starlings' murmuration
in the rose of dusk is the answer.

For the silence of the world
receives every part of you.
So if doubt fills your heart—
listen deeper! The universe is
greeting you with a standing ovation.

reflection questions:
  1. When you call out or pray, how do you listen for an answer?
  2. How do answers come?
  3. Have you ever felt the Universe greeting you with a standing ovation?

SIX: **f r a g m e n t s**

SOFIA
A Fragment of an Unfinished Poem to Laura's
Baby Granddaughter:

Granddaughter—you came in on the wings
of an August night. And I had dreamed of your eyes
for so many nights before I saw them here.

POEMS LAURA INTENDED TO WRITE AND INCLUDE:

GARDEN OF JOY
EQUUS
WISDOM HOUR
POEM FOR MY FATHER
VENUS POEM
ELEPHANT POEM
GRANDDAUGHTER POEM
WHAT THE WATER KNOWS
ELEMENTS POEMS
LEGACY
WHAT THE ACORN KNOWS
THE SEEING WORLD

PRAISE FOR **River of Awe**

PRAISE FOR **RIVER OF AWE**

Laura and I came to know one another when she was already in her dying days. We danced with the big questions of conscious living and conscious dying, slowly turning toward death as a companion instead of an enemy.

Her poetry, motherhood, her fierce love of life, and the cosmology of the Divine Feminine archetype all weaving through our conversations.

Sometimes she would look at me, surprised, and say "I wrote a poem about that".

Laura was a vessel and gave voice to a Mystery, so vast she could barely hold it in her living, a vastness she grew to understand in her dying.

If you are a seeker drawn to the mystery, allow this beautiful collection of poetry by Laura to be your Companion. It will light the way with awe, wonder and love.

— Birgitta Kastenbaum, Transition Life Coach, Death Midwife/Doula, Grief Tending/Rituals, Home Funeral Guide, Educator/Speaker

We gathered on a mild, sunny afternoon for the celebration of Laura Weaver's life at her mother's home. I had never met her in her physical body, but I was able to experience her spirit that day.

Miraculously, the weather changed as the ceremony began, to a freezing wind blowing snow through the back porch. The red roses, intended for each celebrant in her honor, were scattered in one swift breath. The drumming was silenced and we sat in awe to her passion expressed by nature's force.

We all knew it was Laura. It was her spirit present in full force at her own ceremony. We were so honored to experience the shaman, the priestess, the mother, the poet, and the mystery itself, embodied.

Laura Weaver's poems in her *River of Awe* make the face of the divine feminine, both ancient and modern, visible through overlays of her metaphors of nature with mysteries of body, mind, heart and soul. She gives us visions, dreams and communications with the invisible.

Relations with ancestors of her own tribe open to the human tribe as one. Remembrances of ancient rituals and keen observances of life and nature bring the eternal and infinite to the here and now. The sections of Laura's *River of Awe* show a clear succession of movements through life, from personal to transcendent, that mystics call the path of realization.

The steps of this universal path begin at the separation from source (the Headwaters) and the confrontation of limitation (the Rapids), progress through acceptance (On the Riverbank) and fulfillment (Surrendering to the Flow), and culminate in the inevitable encounter of the infinite, eternal Self (Where the River meets the Sea).

What really seals these poems as a female mythology of the spiritual path are the questions at the end of every poem which were added by her soul sister and mother, Pam Hale.

— Susanna Bair, Co-founder & president of iamHeart, Director of the Mentor Program, Co-author of *Living from the Heart, Energize Your Heart* and *Follow Your Heart.*

Through her poetry, Laura takes us on a journey from humanity's deepest pain, through Earth's magical gifts of creation, to the farthest reaches of the mystery of the cosmos, and beyond, and back to our own still center. The journey of remembering that she speaks so eloquently about invites us to fall in love with Life again and again.

As a grief counselor and spiritual companion, I feel these poems are gems of thought-provoking awakening and seeds of possibility within the chrysalis of dark and fertile, though heart-shattering and painful times. Laura beckons us—through these magical and mystical invitations—to break open our hearts, to embrace and embody the full spectrum of life and then to let it go over and over again.

I am forever grateful for her sharing these stunningly mystical insights and stirring reflections. May her stardust be sprinkled through the hearts of many.

— Robyn Hubbard, D. Min., spiritual companion, grief
counselor, dreamwork guide, and beloved soul sister friend

Laura's words guide with tender vulnerability, reminding us, we need not escape our human condition but embrace it, engage it, roar and moan with it, so authentically and live it all with a liberated soul.

— Tryshe Dhevney, Sound Energy Expert, Author, International
Speaker and Sounds True Crystal Bowl Recording

As a physician confronting my patient's physical challenges and as a twenty-five-year cancer survivor confronting personal emotional challenges, I know of what Laura eloquently speaks. The beauty of her words, the depth of her thoughts, and the call to spirit are important to all of us as we face life. Savor her images; relish her phrases; let her poems enrich your everyday being. This is her exquisite legacy to us.

— Lana Holstein, MD

ACKNOWLEDGMENTS

We give thanks to all those who made it possible to bring this collection of Laura's work into the world.

Michelle Stransky designed the beautiful book cover in collaboration with Laura. Marcia Breece ingeniously took elements of that design and applied them to the graphics introducing each section. Marcia, you did such a beautiful job mirroring the design of Laura's first book, *Luminous*, while making this one its own. And thank you for your editing perseverance as we passed draft after draft back and forth.

This collection was being formed mainly from 2018 onward, in the tougher years of Laura's eight-year journey with breast cancer. She was able to live, work and produce these poems supported by her amazing community of beloveds.

As we look at that community, there are too many names to name. We give thanks to all Laura's family and friends. To her women's group, singing group, Boulder besties, spiritual teachers, healers and advisors, celebrants of powerful ceremony, medical and alternative healers, professional colleagues: you supported Laura's life, healing and work in ways that are truly awe-some. To our beloved death doula and her colleagues, Ojai dear ones, and celebrants of Laura's life in Tucson and Boulder, you know who you are. You are in our hearts forever. Your devotion, patience, loyalty and physical care are all woven into this poetry; look for yourselves in her celebrations of life!

We also give thanks to Laura, the author herself. For from beyond the veil, she has appeared to each of her beloveds in different forms, giving us support as we take inspiration from her. It is such a privilege to bring this work, this legacy, into the world.

Laura's family, 2025

Eventually, all things merge into one,
and a river runs through it.
— Norman Maclean

www.ingramcontent.com/pod-product-compliance
Lightning Source LLC
Chambersburg PA
CBHW021115130626
46554CB00002B/703